Colour the picture and write about it.

....

....

....

....

....

Here are some sounds we know from Books 4c and 5c.
Write the letters and make the sounds.

Make the sounds of the letters and complete the word by each picture:

pig, pen, pencil, picture   rabbit, red, road, room
water, woman, window, wall

Pairs of phonic words

Write one of these words on each line below, to make pairs of words—
jam, fox, can, wet, rag, rug, jar, leg, wall, vine, pen

The pictures will help you.

1 man   van
2 ham
3 pan
4 bag
5 net
6 peg
7 men
8 box
9 mug
10 ball
11 car
12 nine

Write the sentences in the correct places.

The dog gets very wet.
She has lots of pegs.
He has a rag for the car.
A cat is on the red rug.
She puts the milk in the jug.

Make the sounds of the letters and complete the word by each picture:

jam, jelly, jug, jar   key, kettle, king, kitten
van, vase, vine, violin

Write these sentences in the correct places.

It is not hot in the house. She has two pots.
He cut it on a tin. Do you like ham?

1. It is her jam.

2. This is a very big ham.

3. Dan has cut his leg.

4. The sun is hot today.

The sound of letters

Fill in these letters to complete the words below.

p, r, w, j, k, v

1. __all
2. __ig
3. __oom
4. __am
5. __ey
6. __an
7. __en
8. __ug
9. __ettle
10. __iolin
11. __abbit
12. __oman

Write the words in the correct order.

1 at the zebra sees He Zoo. the
1 He sees the zebra at the Zoo.

2 yellow some flowers. has She
2 She _____

3 The tell boy time. can the
3 _____

4 violin. The play girl can the
4 _____

5 garden. This wall is a in a
5 _____

6 baby. woman The has little a
6 _____

Make the sounds of the letters and complete the words by the pictures:
box, fox   yellow   zebra, Zoo   quarter, queen, quill

x

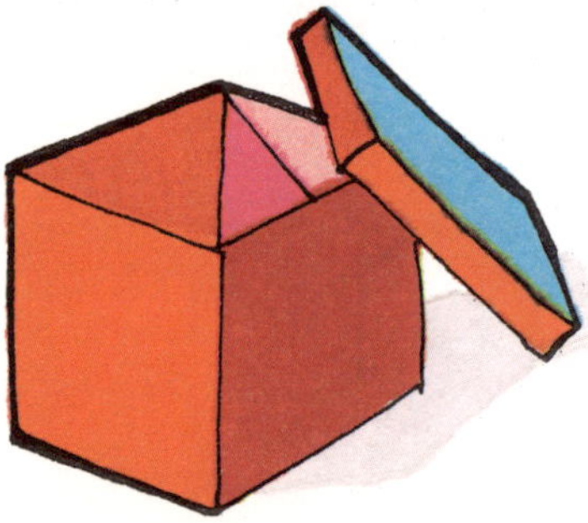

x as in b  _ _   x as in f _ _

y

y for y _ _ _ _ _

z

z for z _ _ _ _ _   and z for Z _ _

qu

qu for qu _ _ _
qu for qu 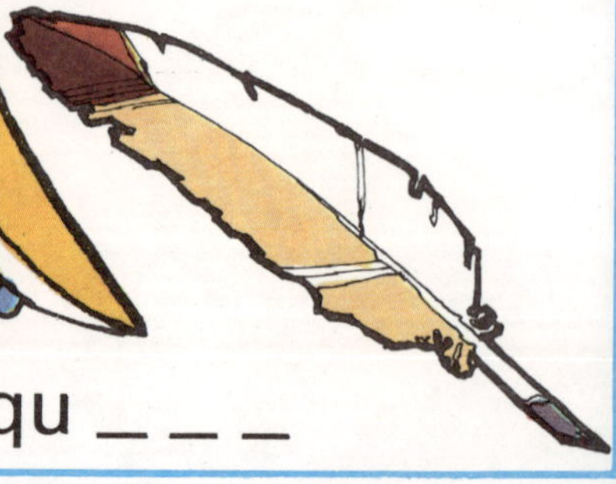 _ _ _ _ _   qu for qu _ _ _

Write these words in their correct places in the sentences below.

1	2	3	4	5	6
one	two	three	four	five	six

1 The boy has _____ ball.
2 The girl has _____ dolls.
3 She has _____ flowers.
4 He has _____ letters.
5 The cat has _____ kittens.
6 The boy has _____ dogs.
7 The woman has _____ eggs.
8 The room has _____ walls.
9 The policeman has _____ keys.
10 The man has _____ cards.

at, by, up, down, in, out, on, under

Write one of the words given above, in each space below:

1 Grandfather is <u>at</u> the door.
2 The kitten is _____ the rug.
3 A man is _____ the van.
4 A jar is _____ the kettle.
5 The boys go _____
6 The fox is going _____
7 The flowers are _____ the vase.
8 Some birds fly _____

The sounds of letters
Fill in these letters to complete the words below:
x, y, z, Z, qu

_ebra

_ _arter

_ellow flower

as in bo_

_oo

_ _een

as in fo_

_ear

Write **Yes** or **No**

Is this a jelly? ....
Is it a quill? ....

Can the fox fly? ....
Can the bird fly? ....

Are there three pencils? ....
Are there six pens? ....

Has she a kitten? ....
Has he a box? ....

Do you like school? ....
Have you a garden? ....

Is the dog very wet? ....
Is she a woman? ....

Write the sentences under the pictures, correctly.

They look round the garden and see the vine.

When it is hot every day, I want to wear a hat.

Pam gave Mr and Mrs Green some eggs.

Peter and Bob have been to find their friend.

Write the sentences by the pictures.

Jane and Molly like their teacher.

Don't jump before you look.

Grandmother gave this to me.

Tell me if you find my pencil.

Write the sentences correctly, by the pictures.

The children go round and round.

If you run you will get hot.

"Don't eat now, dear," says the teacher.

I am going to rub the horse down.

Number the sentences to match the pictures.

○ The Queen sits next to the King.

○ "Don't do that," he says.

○ The ball is in the road.

○ "Look before you get it," she says.

Look for these in the two pictures below.
Write the name of each one under the picture in which you can see it.

a chair   some birds   a tree   a jar   a jug
a woman   some flowers   a baby   a gate   a window
a vase   some jam   the sun   a jelly   a door
a violin   a nest   an umbrella   a cat   a rug

1 a chair

2

3

4

5

6

7

8

9

10

1 some birds

2

3

4

5

6

7

8

9

10

The boy was in danger in the water.

Colour the picture.

They get the boy into the boat.

Write the words.

Tom pulls the boy out of the water.

Tom _____

The boy is about nine years old.

T _____

He wants his own mother and father.

H _____

Jane does her best for the boy.

J _____

Tom asks, "Where is your home?"

T _____

Write about these pictures, on the page opposite.

Write these sentences in the right order, to match the pictures opposite.

Two boys run up to help Dan.

He sits by the water for some time.

The boys pull Dan out of the water.

Dan is going to fish today.

At home Dan tells the others about it.

Now Dan is in the water.

1 _____

2 _____

3 _____

4 _____

5 _____

6 _____

Write these words in the correct places, under the pictures:

It has been in the water.
They are by the window.
are Mr and Mrs Green.
He is under it as he works.

He rubs the dog as it is wet.

Father's friend helps with the car.

The Queen sits next to the King.

The father and mother

Write the sentences in the correct places.

Peter finds a very big apple.
"This one is much the best,"
he says.

Grandfather is Mother's father.
Grandmother is Mother's mother.

He has a quarter of the cake
and a mug of tea.

Pam has Ann, the doll.
"I like your doll, Jane,"
she says.

Mother's friend helps
with the pots and pans
before going home.

Fill in the missing words from this list:

been, their, live, door, loves, much, lot, jelly, writes, friend, When, hat

1. Ann and Bob have _____ to the sea with _____ friends.
2. They _____ next _____ to each other.
3. She lives here because she _____ trees so _____.
4. The big boy has a _____ of _____.
5. Jane _____ a letter to her _____. "Dear Mary," she writes.
6. He comes every day. _____ it is hot he has a _____.

Write about the picture.

....

....

....

....

....

Each year Grandfather takes the children to the Zoo.

They walk round for some time, and then have something to eat.

Here is Peter on an elephant. Jane looks at an ostrich.

They have a good time at the Zoo.

Reading test

pen pencil road room woman window wall wet jam fox rag rug jar vine van pan peg box mug very lot jug jelly key kettle king kitten hot pots today violin zebra zoo yellow tell time garden baby quarter queen quill three four six dolls eggs grandfather door vase birds fly year round when every day hat Pam gave Mr Mrs Green Bob been find their friend Molly teacher don't before grandmother if dear am rub next Tom old own mother father does best your much Ann lives because loves Mary